The *GOLF Magazine*
Short Game
Handbook

Other titles in the series

The *GOLF Magazine* Golf Fitness Handbook
The *GOLF Magazine* Mental Golf Handbook
The *GOLF Magazine* Course Management Handbook
The *GOLF Magazine* Full Swing Handbook
The *GOLF Magazine* Putting Handbook

The *GOLF Magazine* Short Game Handbook

Peter Morrice
and the Editors of *GOLF Magazine*

Photography by Sam Greenwood

The Lyons Press

First Lyons Press edition, 2000

Printed in the United States of America
Design and composition by Compset, Inc.

10 9 8 7 6 5 4 3 2 1

The Library of Congress Cataloging-in-Publication Data

Morrice, Peter.
    The Golf magazine short game handbook/Peter
Morrice and the editors of Golf magazine; illustrated
by Sam Greenwood.
        p. cm.
    ISBN: 1–55821–938–2
    1. Short game (Golf)—Handbooks, manuals, etc.
  I. Title: Short game handbook. II. Title

GV979.S54 M67 2000
796.352'3—dc21
                                        99-086543

Acknowledgments

Many people contributed to the making of this book. First, my gratitude to George Peper, editor-in-chief of *GOLF Magazine*, who trusted this project in my hands. And to Bryan Oettel and Jill Hindle at The Lyons Press, whose editorial skills and professionalism made them perfect partners. For the photographs, I thank *GOLF Magazine* staff photographer Sam Greenwood, as well as Mike Stubblefield, Dennis Blake, Mike LaBrutto, and Wendy Obenrader, who modeled for and helped with the photo shoots. Lastly, a big thanks to my family and friends for their patience and constant encouragement during late nights and long weekends. Special recognition goes to my parents: my father for the golf, my mother for the writing.

Contents

Foreword by George Peper, GOLF Magazine 11

Introduction 17

Chipping 21

    What Is a Chip? 23

    When Not to Chip 25

    How to Plan a Chip 28

    Chipping Setup 31

    Chipping Swing 35

    Common Faults 41

    Chipping Variations 47

    The Bump-and-Run. 47

The Super-Short Chip 49

Chipping from Poor Lies 51

Pitching 57

What Is a Pitch? 59

When Not to Pitch 62

How to Plan a Pitch 64

Pitching Setup 67

Pitching Swing 73

Common Faults 83

Pitching Variations 86

The Lob Shot 86

The Half-Wedge 89

Hilly Lies 91

Deep Rough 93

Sand Play 97

How to Plan a Bunker Shot 99

Bunker Setup 103

Bunker Swing 109

Common Faults 116

Bunker-Shot Variations 118

Specialty Shots 125

   The Bellied Wedge 129

   The Wood Chip. 131

   The Bunker Putt. 133

   The Banker 136

   The Grassy Blast 139

   The Hook Chip 141

   The Trap Shot 144

   The Half-Grass, Half-Sand Shot. 146

Practice 149

   The Short of It. 151

   Make It Real 154

   Make It Fun. 156

   The Rewards of Hard Work 158

Foreword

At *GOLF Magazine* we use two methods to determine the content to include each month: surveys and guts. In the survey method, questionnaires are sent to thousands of our subscribers, asking what topics they enjoy most, which kinds of articles they prefer, etc. In the guts method, we editors simply use our intuition as kindred, hopelessly addicted golfers.

But no matter which method we use, the number-one answer is always the same: instruction. "Give us more instruction," has been the mandate from our readers ever since the magazine began publishing forty years ago. The reason is simple: A golfer is happiest when his game is improving.

Recently, however, we've learned a couple of things about how to present our instruction. Number one, you like it short and sweet. After all, most of the current populace was raised on television, sound bites, and quick delivery of information, from beepers to e-mail. More than ever, we like our messages short and to the point.

And the "to the point" part is just as important as the "short" part. For the last decade or so, the most popular portion of *GOLF Magazine* has been the buff-colored section called "Private Lessons," which brings together custom-tailored instruction for five different kinds of golfers: low handicappers, high handicappers, short but straight hitters, long but crooked hitters, and senior golfers. In this way, we're able to speak more personally to our readers and help them more individually with their games.

Why am I telling you all this? Because the same kind of thinking went into the book that is now in your hands. When the people at The Lyons Press came to talk to us about a partnership in golf book publishing, we gave them our mantra for success: instruction, succinct and focused. The result is the *GOLF Magazine* series of guides, each written concisely, edited mercilessly, and dedicated entirely to one key aspect of playing the game.

Each *GOLF Magazine* guide assembles a wealth of great advice in a package small enough to carry in your golf bag. We hope you'll use these pages to raise your game to a whole new level.

George Peper
Editor-in-Chief
GOLF Magazine

The *GOLF Magazine* Short Game Handbook

Introduction

What's the big deal about the short game? Green-side shots are not that hard to execute and even if you do totally bungle them, the consequences aren't exactly devastating. I mean, when's the last time you chipped a ball out of bounds or lost your Saturday Nassau on a poor bunker shot. Never, right?

Well, yes and no. You see, the short game—chipping, pitching, bunker shots, and the like—is stuck between the flashiness of the full swing and the finality of putting. After all, every hole starts with a tee shot and finishes with a putt. Errors around the green aren't as obvious because they're neither as dramatic as full-swing errors, where the ball can fly 40 or 50 yards off-line, nor as definitive as putting errors, which seem to make the difference between bogeys and pars, between the 80s and the 90s.

But the short game has hidden significance. For instance, when you chip from the fringe to eight feet then miss the putt for par, do you blame poor putting for a failed up-and-down? Probably. Would you dwell on a topped tee shot or a chunked chip after making a double bogey? Chances are, you'll remember that humiliating drive for the rest of the day. This is human nature: We want pretty shots and low scores. In the mix, golfers lose sight of the short game—the shots that allow them to recover from that poor drive or make that makable putt . . . well, *makable.*

Think of how many holes you play during a typical round without using your wedges, without chipping or pitching or blasting your way onto the green. Not many, I bet. And if you're using those wedges two or three times a hole, that's a good indication that your short game needs help. That's okay; most short games do. The real problem is that most golfers don't really analyze this part of their game, certainly not like they do their golf swing.

This book invites you to do just that—and then to do something about it. In the pages that follow you will find all the setup and swing keys for playing the standard chip, pitch, and bunker shots, as well as many other "specialty shots." You'll also find tips on greenside decision-making, strategy, the mental game, and how to best use your practice time. In addition, tips from Tour pros and many of *GOLF Magazine*'s Top 100 Teachers are included in a recurring feature called "Best Tip." Assembled from the archives of *GOLF Magazine*, these represent the finest short-game tips we've come across in our forty years of publishing golf instruction.

So, with some of the know-how presented in this book, and a little practice, you can dramatically improve your play around the greens. It really is up to you.

Chipping

Let's put some meaning to the "short" in short game. Here's the number-one rule in greenside play: Produce the "shortest" ball flight with the "shortest" possible swing that allows you to get the ball to the hole.

And what does that mean? It means keep the swing simple and get the ball rolling as soon as possible. If you can commit this concept to memory and recall it often, you'll save yourself countless strokes around the green. And that means lower scores, the quest for which no doubt has led you to this book.

Okay, so it's not quite that simple. Let me attach two conditions to our "short" philosophy. First, although you want the shortest ball flight, you should land the ball on the green whenever possible, where you'll get the most predictable bounce. Shoot to land the ball a yard or two onto the putting surface to allow some room for error on the short side.

The second condition involves the length of the swing. You want it to be as short as it can be, provided you maintain a smooth, natural rhythm from start to finish. In other words, don't make your backswing so short that you have to jerk the club on your downswing to get enough power. If you feel as if you have to help the club back down, your backswing is too short.

Let this rule, with its two conditions, guide your greenside play. If you do, you'll soon discover that most short shots can be run along the ground. Simply put, chipping is the backbone of the short game. It's the highest percentage play you can make, driven by a simple single-lever motion, with the left arm and the club essentially staying in a straight line from setup to finish. The swing is short and repeatable, and the ball flies low and rolls most of the way to the hole.

It's fitting that our analysis start with the standard chip shot. It may not be the most exciting shot in the game, but it is the easiest to learn and the safest to employ. In the words of the immortal Bobby Jones, "The chip is the great economist of golf."

What Is a Chip?

The first step in becoming a smarter, more effective player around the greens is understanding your options, understanding the difference between a chip, a pitch, a lob, and so on. Once you know the characteristics of each shot, you can confidently choose among them in a given situation, knowing that you have picked the right play. Such confidence breeds success.

The chip shot is generally thought to be any short shot that flies no more than a third of its total distance and rolls at least two thirds. Keep in mind these are the outside parameters that apply when chipping with a wedge; chips played with a short or middle iron can roll as much as five or six times farther than they carry in the air.

The chip shot comes with little risk. Its objective is to bump the ball out of the grass and onto the edge of the green. Except for a putt, it's the simplest motion in golf, and the simpler the motion, the less the chance of something going wrong. Add this to

The chip shot rolls at least two-thirds of its total distance.

the fact that a rolling ball is more predictable than a flying ball that can still take a bad hop when it lands, and you'll understand why the chip should be your first greenside choice.

The putting stroke is even safer, but putting from off the green requires an excellent lie and smooth ground the whole way. Otherwise, the chip is a better bet. Remember, your objective should be to minimize risk: Putt before you chip; chip before you pitch; pitch before you lob. Keep that in mind and you're on your way to getting the most out of your game around the greens.

When Not to Chip

For all its good qualities, there are times when a chip shot is the wrong choice. If you have to carry the ball more than a third of the way to the hole due to intervening obstacles, such as deep rough or sand, you should play a more lofted shot. The worst swing thought you can have around the green is that you have to help the ball into the air to land safely on the green. When this notion crosses your mind, stop and rethink your shot.

Likewise, when hitting to an elevated green, you may need more height than a standard chip provides to carry the ball onto the putting surface. Try-

BEST TIP: Grip-Down Drill

Good chipping demands firm wrists through impact and free body rotation back and through. To ingrain these fundamentals, practice your chipping motion with your hands choked down to the shaft and the butt of the grip touching your left side. Keeping the grip against your ribs, swing the clubhead back and through in the air, noting how your wrists remain stable and your body turns back and through with the swinging motion.

—Carl Welty, *GOLF Magazine* Top 100 Teacher

ing to bounce your ball into or up a slope is unpredictable. Plan your first bounce to be on the putting surface itself, where the ground usually is more level and the grass is uniform.

Sometimes a poor lie in deep rough also makes a chip shot inadvisable, since the ball needs to come out high enough to keep from getting snagged by the long grass. In fact, even when the ball itself is sitting up, the grass around it must be considered: A clump of thick grass behind the ball may require a steeper downswing than the standard chip provides, and long grass in front of the ball may require a higher launch angle off the clubface.

BEST TIP: Learn to rotate your body and keep your wrists firm by choking up on a club and swinging with the grip against your left side.

So, the chip shot is not the be-all and end-all of the short game, but it should be your favorite option around the green. Whenever putting is unwise—and it often is—set your sights on chipping. If you can't make a strong case *against* chipping, you have a strong case *for* it.

How to Plan a Chip

Chip-shot execution should begin as soon as your previous shot comes to rest. Say you've missed your approach shot to the right and your ball finds an uphill lie just off a slick downhill green. The best view of this shot is probably on your walk up to the green: You can see the nature of the terrain from start to finish, where the ball should land, the incline of the lie, and the decline of the green. These subtleties are tough to judge once you're at the ball. Take full advantage of your perspective on your walk to the green.

Once you reach the ball, develop a picture in your mind as to how you want the shot to look: the bounce, the roll, the final destination. Crouch down behind the ball and read the shot like you would a putt, first picking a spot on the green for the initial bounce. Remember, this landing spot should be at least a yard onto the green to provide room for error if you catch the shot a bit heavy or thin.

Next comes club selection. There are two schools of thought on how to pick a club for chipping. One theory says develop a comfort level with a single club, say a pitching wedge, and use it for all your chip shots, adjusting the length of the swing to dictate the distance of the shot. The other theory advocates a single swing for chipping that produces different shots with different clubs, anything from a sand wedge to a 5-iron. Both are reliable methods, although changing clubs rather than adjusting your swing to produce different results is a simpler approach.

We'll get into the mechanics of the setup and swing in a moment, but first consider two preshot factors that grow in importance as you get closer to the hole: precision and relaxation. Simply put, the shorter the shot, the greater your expectation of precision. For example, if you miss a green with a 3-iron, you may not be all that upset; but if you leave a little chip shot in the long grass, you want to bite the club in half. That's because you've fallen miserably short of your expectations.

As for relaxation, shorter shots require less big-muscle motion and therefore rely more on your sense of rhythm and timing. Tension is rhythm's

To bolster feel, make swings looking down the line.

biggest enemy, making it critical to ward off stress on short shots. To do this, commit to the shot and club you've chosen and focus on executing what you see in your mind's eye. Make a few rehearsal swings in a similar lie, looking down the line and sensing the effort required, then step up and hit the ball. Don't waste time second-guessing your decisions. Extra time means extra tension. Envision, commit, rehearse, and execute.

Chipping Setup

The basic motion of the chip shot is a downward hit, the clubface contacting the ball before the club has reached the bottom of its downswing arc. This descending action is preferred because the most important factor in chipping is clean clubface-to-ball contact, and the most reliable method for doing this is making contact while the clubhead is still in its descent. Think of it as pinching the ball against the turf.

Clean contact in chipping is critical for two reasons: First, catching grass before the ball on a chipping swing kills the momentum of the clubhead, often cutting power significantly before it reaches the ball; and second, when grass gets trapped be-

---

Free Chips

Next time you're walking down the fairway with your wedge in hand, stop for a minute and take a few practice chipping swings, trying to brush a leaf or loose grass off the turf. You'll be surprised how smooth and rhythmic your stroke is without the prospect of a difficult shot in front of you. Try to internalize this fluid action and recall it the next time you face an intimidating chip shot.

tween the clubface and the ball, the nature of the contact and the spin imparted on the ball is unpredictable. Catching grass first may work out on full shots, where the clubhead often tears through the grass with little effect, but when playing from short range, you simply cannot take the chance of making poor contact.

Every aspect of the standard chipping setup is designed to promote a descending blow and a low, running shot that lands just on the green and rolls to the hole. Here are the specifics:

Play the ball back.   Position the ball opposite your right instep and push your hands toward the target, until they're even with your left thigh. This hands-ahead position sets up a steep backswing and a descending motion at impact, with the hands leading the clubhead until well after the ball is gone.

Set your weight left.   Place 60 to 70 percent of your body weight on your left foot at address. This further encourages a downward angle of approach but also discourages weight transfer during the swing by presetting the weight on the target side, where it has to end up. Weight transfer is an unnecessary complication in chipping.

For a standard chip, set the ball back and your weight left.

Take a narrow stance.   With your heels six to eight inches apart, you'll naturally resist weight movement during the swing. Keeping the feet close together also sets you more upright and therefore nearer the ball, which increases your control of the motion, as your hands and arms stay closer to the body.

Choke down for feel.   Slide your hands down the grip until your right hand is almost to the end of the handle. This effectively shortens the club, which reduces the power of the swing and bolsters control.

Set up square to slightly open.   A square stance makes sense, as it promotes a straight clubhead path through impact, but some golfers like to open up a bit to gain a better view of the line. This is a matter of preference: If you feel comfortable standing open, it can be beneficial, but if you find yourself hitting chips off-line, by all means use a square setup.

Square the clubface.   As you move the ball back in your stance, the tendency will be to flare the clubface open. And unless you make an in-swing compensation, you all but guarantee an open clubface at impact, which will send the ball right of your intended line. To guard against this, always make sure the leading edge, or bottom, of your clubface is perpendicular to your starting line, regardless of ball position. Then you can swing away knowing your clubface will be square when it meets the ball.

BEST TIP: Looking Ahead

In chipping, a slight lean toward the target at address promotes a steep downswing and clean contact with the ball. To create this leaning action, focus your eyes on the front half of the ball as you take your stance. This will ensure that your head is slightly in front of the ball and that the shaft is angled toward the target. From there, the backswing will be fairly upright, setting up a descending blow and crisp contact.

—Laird Small, *GOLF Magazine* Top 100 Teacher

Chipping Swing

You've no doubt heard the term "one-piece takeaway" to describe the first move away from the ball in the full swing. Well, this concept of starting the

arms, shoulders, and club in a unified, synchronized motion is a great mental image for the chipping swing as well—not only on the takeaway, but
throughout the entire motion.

Picture the chipping setup just described or, better yet, take your address facing a full-length mirror. You'll notice your arms and shoulders form a
large triangle—each arm being a side and the line
of your shoulders representing the third side. The
key to good chipping is keeping this triangle intact
from the setup to the finish, meaning it should not
change shape as you swing away from the ball or
through to the target. This demands that the shoulders turn at the same rate that the arms swing.

The age-old concept that chipping is a hands-and-
arms motion is dead wrong. The small muscles of
the hands, wrists, and forearms are the least reliable
actors in the golf swing, particularly under pressure,
and therefore should be prohibited from leading
any motion. Instead, think of the chipping swing as
a mini-turn back and a mini-turn through—a one-
piece motion all the way.

Here's the basic technique for chipping:

Start relaxed.   Tension in the hands, arms, or
body at address virtually guarantees a quick start,

from which a chipping swing will rarely recover. To prevent tension and encourage a smooth first move, hover the clubhead at address, slowly wagging it back and forth as you track your eyes down the line. Watch Raymond Floyd, one of the game's best chippers, as he stands over chip shots; he looks as if he's drawing circles in the air with his clubhead.

Swing triangle back.   Keeping your weight left and your head stock-still, move the hands, arms, and shoulders away from the ball as a single unit. This is a pendulum-type motion similar to putting, where no part of the swing outraces any other and the body center stays firmly in place.

Let the body react.   Although you shouldn't consciously hinge your wrists during the chipping swing, they should be free to react naturally to the swinging of the club. This will happen automatically if you keep your grip soft. As for your lower body, it should also feel relaxed and responsive. The knees and hips should rotate back slightly in reaction to the swinging motion, without any thought on your part.

The arms and shoulders swing the club back together.

Reverse the motion.　　The downswing should be a mirror image of the backswing. If you've started from a good setup position, you need not think about making the downward blow required in chipping. Simply swing the arms-and-shoulders triangle to the target, letting the clubhead naturally accelerate through impact.

Let the clubhead accelerate through the strike.

Finish to the target. Assuming you have a decent lie, there should be nothing choppy in your chipping motion. Swing the clubhead through at least as far as you swung it back, never letting your wrists flip or your shoulders stop rotating. At the finish, the clubhead should be about shin-high and your upper body should be half-turned toward the target.

Follow through with the club and your body.

Common Faults

Chipping should be a piece of cake. The motion is only slightly more complicated than a long putt, yet many amateurs struggle to even make solid contact on chip shots, sending them half or twice their intended distance. If they were to do that in putting, they'd find something else to do on Saturday mornings.

Unfortunately, many golfers have learned to live with—even expect—poor chipping. They've dismissed it as an aspect of the game that requires a degree of touch or finesse they simply don't possess. Fact is, the motion is so simple, most problems stem more from a misunderstanding of the technique than from mechanical errors that occur during the swing.

We know the number-one requirement of effective chipping is clean contact with the ball. Why, then, do so many amateurs set up with the ball forward in their stance and their weight centered or even favoring their rear foot? These positions scream trouble. If the body is set behind the ball, a crisp, downward blow is difficult to produce, leaving the clubhead little chance of meeting the ball without first catching grass. The result is usually poor contact and therefore poor distance control.

BEST TIP: Keep It Up

Hitting chip shots fat from greenside rough is a common problem that often results when golfers sole the clubhead behind the ball at address. You see, grounding the clubhead in effect establishes the touchdown point of the swing: If you start with the clubhead resting behind the ball, you'll tend to swing it into the ground at that spot, producing contact behind the ball. To prevent this, hover the clubhead above the grass at address, setting up a downward swing into the ball and good contact.

—Jim Flick, *GOLF Magazine*
Master Teaching Professional

To make sure you're setting up correctly, focus on two things: playing the ball off your right instep and leaning the shaft toward the target, so the butt of the grip points at your left hip. With your hands well ahead of the ball at address, you're virtually guaranteed to make a descending blow, putting the clubface on the ball without any interference. Getting the setup right is more than half the battle in chipping: The swing is so short and simple, it has little chance to slip off-track.

BEST TIP: Hover the clubhead above the ground at address to promote crisp contact with the ball.

Setting the weight right usually leads to poor contact.

Aside from a faulty setup, many golfers have a poor understanding of how the chipping motion should feel. Perhaps the most harmful piece of advice on this subject is "chip like you putt." Players who try to do this tend to rock their shoulders stiffly up and down, instead of letting them rotate around the spine as they do for every other golf shot. This rocking action makes the upper body tip toward the target on the backswing and away on the downswing, which changes the bottom of the swing arc and leads to fat chips or contact on the upswing.

Other golfers don't let the shoulders move at all. In an attempt to keep the body perfectly still, they swing the club with only their hands and arms, letting the wrists hinge and the hands take control. Problem is, when the hands dictate the backswing, they also control the downswing and that means unpredictable bursts of speed and inconsistent contact.

Chipping Ratios

GOLF Magazine Top 100 Teachers Paul Runyan and Phil Rodgers developed a system of carry-to-roll ratios of chip shots hit with various clubs. For instance, the carry-to-roll relationship of a standard 9-iron chip is three parts roll for every one part flight. Here are the ratios for the common chipping clubs:

Club	Carry : Roll
6-iron	1 : 6
7-iron	1 : 5
8-iron	1 : 4
9-iron	1 : 3
Pitching wedge	1 : 2

If you try to "chip like you putt," you'll make a stiff, mechanical swing.

To correct these faulty motions, think of the chipping swing as the golf swing in miniature. When the arms swing, the shoulders must turn, and nothing should be forced not to move. Forced actions mean tension, and tension kills feel. If you think you're a bad chipper, you're probably just getting in your own way. Remember, relax and keep it natural.

Chipping Variations

While there are conditions that make chipping inadvisable, such as limited green to work with or intervening obstacles, you're often better off adapting your chipping technique slightly than selecting a riskier play. Think of the chip as your default shot: If you can't eliminate it as a viable option, it's the right choice. Consider adding these variations of the chip shot to your short-game arsenal.

The Bump-and-Run

On standard greenside chip shots, landing the ball on the green is a top priority, but there are situations when bouncing the ball short is an acceptable play. The bump-and-run, which is essentially a long chip shot, is designed to land well short of the green and bounce several times before reaching the putting surface. It can cover anywhere from 20 to 100 yards, depending on the club used and the length of the swing (experiment with different clubs to get a feel for distance). But for this to be a wise play, you need to have a firm, unimpeded path to the hole.

The bump-and-run can be effective if you have a clear path.

The technique for the bump-and-run is similar to the chip shot, with two exceptions: The ball is played in the middle of the stance, not back; and the wrists are allowed to hinge a little more to lengthen the swing. But the motion looks a lot like a long chip: Arms and shoulders move back and through together, the lower body only reacting to the movement of the arms and upper body. Using anything from an 8-iron to a 4-iron, try to clip the ball off the turf with a level, sweeping motion, imparting minimal backspin so the ball bounds forward after landing.

The Super-Short Chip

At the other end of the spectrum from the bump-and-run is the super-short chip shot. This shot is useful in those pesky situations when your ball lies in long grass just off the green and the hole is cut very close to you. You need to bump the ball out—just a few feet—and stop it quickly.

In this situation, most amateurs grab their sand wedge and try to flip the ball over the long grass. In all honesty, that requires more touch and coordination than most golfers can muster. The usual result is either a fat or skulled shot. A better plan is to pop the ball out with a modified chipping motion, keep-

On super-short chip shots, cut across the ball to deaden the hit.

ing the swing simple and limiting the chance for disaster.

Using your sand or lob wedge, open your stance and play the ball off your right instep. Then open the clubface so it points slightly right of the target. From there, simply swing the clubhead back along your stance line, keeping your wrists firm, and try to slide the clubface under the ball. Forget about the follow-through; focus on making the clubface point to the sky after impact. Your objective is to cut across the ball, imparting a weak blow that pops the ball onto the green without enough energy to get away from you.

Chipping from Poor Lies

You simply cannot predict how the clubhead will react if it catches grass, not to mention ground, before it meets the ball. The chipping swing does not have enough energy to lose horsepower before impact and still produce a decent shot. In effect, you either hit it cleanly or you're hitting it again.

Let's look at a few lies that require special consideration. How about when your ball is sitting in a patch of thick, clumpy rough? To create the contact you need, make a more upright backswing to avoid

getting the clubhead caught in the grass and to promote a steep descent to the ball.

To accomplish this, play the ball farther back in
your stance at address—off your right toe or even

Out of thick grass, play the ball farther back in your
stance and set more weight left.

the outside of your right foot. Be sure to set your weight left and start with your hands well ahead of the ball. This setup promotes the steep up-and-down motion you need from this lie. Keep in mind also that playing the ball back delofts the clubface, making a pitching wedge play like a 7- or 8-iron. Club down accordingly.

You must make similar adjustments when playing from muddy or hardpan lies. In both cases, there is no room for error in the contact department—a premature touchdown means a chunked shot. On hardpan, the clubhead will sometimes ricochet off the ground and into the middle of the ball, producing a skulled shot. Either way, the results are disastrous.

To handle such lies, select an 8- or 9-iron, play the ball in line with the outside of the right foot, and set most of your weight on your left side—even more so than when playing from thick rough. Understand that the farther back the ball and the more weight you have on your left, the steeper the swing will be, without any hinging of the wrists. From extremely firm lies, try to pinch the back of the ball against the ground. The combination of a steep downward hit and firm ground to hit against will produce lots of backspin; expect the ball to bounce a few times and check up quickly.

Sometimes a ball rolls into a perched lie on top of the grass. Good contact may seem like a no-brainer from here, but you still need to allow for a different kind of impact. These lies create cushion under the ball, as the grass, not the ground, is supporting the ball's weight. If you hit down with a standard chipping motion, the clubface will either sink in the grass, causing weak contact on the top of the clubface, or the ball will dive down into the grass before popping out. In both instances, the ball will come out weakly, and you'll feel as if you've wasted a great opportunity.

BEST TIP: Aim for Hollows

Traditional instruction says to land your greenside shots on flat areas of the green whenever possible. However, if you can plan a shot that will land in the middle of a dip or hollow, go for it. If you land short, the downslope will kick the ball forward, making up for your lack of carry. Hit the ball a little too long and you'll catch the upslope on the far side of the dip, slowing its progress. Total distance for all three shots—landing in the middle, short, or long—will be about the same, providing the largest possible margin for error.

—Dave Pelz, *GOLF Magazine* Technical and
Short Game Consultant

Take advantage of this teed-up lie by hitting the ball with a more level or sweeping motion, much like a long putting stroke. Play the ball in the middle of your stance and position your eyes directly over it. From there, make a simple arms-and-shoulders swing back and through, keeping the wrists firm. The ball will pop forward with little backspin, due to the level impact angle, and roll smoothly to the hole.

When the ball is sitting up, make a level, sweeping motion.

Pitching

Be honest now: When you think of someone who has a great short game—whether it's Tiger Woods or your regular weekend partner—you're thinking about how he lofts the ball high in the air and drops it dead to the hole, right? You don't care much about the running shot; heck, you can skull a sand wedge and make it run. But the guy who can get some air under the ball—there's a guy who has some short-game savvy.

Well, this kind of thinking is a reality of modern golf. The player with a showy short game, who plays it high when he could go low, who makes that long wristy swing when he could play a standard chip shot, is the player who will get the reputation as a whiz around the greens. There's some-

thing innately cool about missing a green and floating a shot from the edge of disaster to three feet—
and doing it five times a round. But mostly, people
love such players because they feel they could
never be one.

The general feeling among amateurs, it seems, is
that you basically have it or you don't when it
comes to hitting high-lofted, soft-landing shots.
You're either blessed with "good hands" and the
moxie to take on difficult situations, or you want to
run and hide every time a shot calls for a little finesse. Unfortunately, most golfers would put themselves in the latter group.

Given that fact, it's amazing that so many golfers
are quick to grab their sand or lob wedge and try to
loft the ball at every opportunity. This is a great
irony: Players who have no confidence in their
greenside touch routinely choose high-lofted shots
over low-risk running shots. It's as if they have no
memory of their track record around the greens.

In most instances, they choose the shot they'd
like to play, not the one they should play. They mis-
interpret the old adage "To be a great player you
have to think like a great player." That doesn't
mean attempting shots that are way over your head
(literally) but playing the best shot, given the situation and your skill level. There are plenty of Tour

pros making millions with chinks in their short-game armor. The secret is knowing where those weak spots are and playing away from them.

But pitching the ball in the air is neither as difficult nor as mysterious as many people make it out to be. Becoming a good pitcher starts with a basic understanding of the physics of a golf shot and the design characteristics of the clubs you're using. Are some golfers naturally better than you around the greens? Sure they are; that's life. But you can get better.

What Is a Pitch?

The basic objective of a pitch shot is to get the ball into the air quickly to carry obstacles that stand between you and the hole, obstacles such as bunkers, deep rough, or water. The other end of the shot, after the ball lands safely on the green, requires a soft bounce and a quick stop, as the ball has already flown a good way to the hole.

This second part of the equation takes care of itself. You see, a high-lofted shot lands at a steeper angle to the ground, causing it to bounce more upward than forward. When this happens, the energy of the shot is exerted downward upon landing and absorbed by the ground, producing a weak rebound and little forward momentum.

In terms of flight-to-roll ratios, the pitch takes over where the chip leaves off: The chip is *no more than* one third flight, while the pitch is *at least* one third flight. A standard pitch with a pitching wedge is generally thought to be about half flight and half roll.

The pitch has become more and more popular as courses have become better manicured and heavily irrigated, leading to better lies and added stopping power on the greens. Our forebears in the game had little use for the pitch shot, as the greens of those days were far too firm to accept even a high-lofted pitch. But today's golfers can fly shots well into a green and be reasonably confident they will come to rest without rolling over. And since any well-executed pitch carries trouble and sits down quickly, it appears to be low risk. This is simply not true: Loft means risk.

When most golfers see thick rough or sand between them and the green, they think one thing: "Gotta get over that stuff." Loft seems the obvious issue, but the lie of the ball is even more important, as it dictates how cleanly you can make contact. As you'll see, a standard pitch requires at least a decent lie and a longer, more complicated swing than the chip. The more things you have to factor in to a swing, the more things can go wrong; there is less

The pitch shot flies higher and rolls less than the chip.

room for error. This is the case with high-lofted shots, which makes them risky. Golfers lose sight of that, and they pay dearly for it.

BEST TIP: Aiming High

To hit higher pitch shots, open the clubface to increase its effective loft. However, since the ball flies in the direction the clubface points, you have to make a corresponding move or else lose these shots to the right. To properly add loft, rotate the clubface open, then take your grip and shift your stance to the left until the clubface points back to the target.

—Mike Adams, *GOLF Magazine*
Top 100 Teacher

When Not to Pitch

Think of pitching as a necessary evil. There are times around the green when the chip shot would fly too low or run too far to fit the situation. This is when the higher-risk pitch shot should be considered, but not before.

When should you pitch? Since a chip is maximum one third flight, and you want to land the ball on the green to ensure a predictable bounce, your green light for pitching comes whenever you can't chip the ball onto the green with your highest lofted chipping club. For instance, if you can't chip the ball onto the green with your sand wedge, it's time to consider the pitch.

Once you opt to pitch the ball, select the least lofted club you can to play the shot, always trying to maximize ground time. Keep in mind, as loft increases, your swing length must also increase to cover the same distance because the swing's energy is sending the ball both upward and outward. The greater upward force means a weaker outward force, and hence a shot that travels less distance.

Don't forget about roll. As you add loft, realize you are also taking away roll, due to the steeper angle of descent to the ground. See how the risk factor is escalating? Hitting the ball higher means you have to carry it closer to the hole, bringing your margin for error on the far side of the

Fly High, Stop Fast

If you're like most golfers, you're amazed when the pros drop a pitch shot next to the hole, bounce it twice, and draw it back like a yo-yo. You'd love to be able to make the ball stop like that. Trouble is, you probably don't play a soft enough ball to create that much backspin. Instead, when you have to stop the ball quickly, simply hit a higher shot that plops straight down with little forward momentum. It's a safer, more dependable way than adding backspin to make the ball stop in its tracks.

green into the picture: A slight mishit may spell big trouble over the back.

How to Plan a Pitch

In golf, great pitchers can eye up a situation, grab a wedge, and dial in the shot they need. This skill has nothing to do with natural ability: It comes from experience and practice. Nobody picks up golf with a knack for pitching the ball accurate distances; it results from planning and executing thousands of pitch shots until you learn to match the situation you see with the motion you've learned. To be sure, it's an art, not a science.

The shot process in pitching starts with a careful assessment of the situation at hand—the slope of the terrain, any obstacles to negotiate, and the quality of the lie. As with chipping, you should start to evaluate the shot on your trek to the green. As you approach, you'll face the first set of critical questions: Where should you land the ball? Any trouble at the far side? Where do you want to putt from? Such questions are often best answered from a panoramic perspective.

However, the lie of the ball stands above all others in the analysis of a pitch shot. Pitching features less of a descending blow than chipping, which means the grass behind the ball comes into play to a much greater degree. If you try to hit a standard pitch from a buried lie in the rough, you're likely to catch a clubface full of grass before the ball, resulting in a weak shot. Try to develop a sense for what to expect from various lies and how to handle them. Again, that comes with experience.

Okay, after considering the above factors, you've decided you're going to pitch the ball; now you need the right club. More specifically, you need the right wedge, as all your pitching should be done with a wedge. Why? Two reasons: First, you need the higher loft that the wedges provide; and second, the more lofted the club, the heavier the flange (bottom of the clubhead) and therefore the lower the center of gravity. Both of these design features help you slide the leading edge of the clubface under the ball at impact, producing a high, soft shot.

How do you know which wedge to use? Well, that's a personal decision. More loft may create a higher percentage play, if, for instance, it gives you more room for error in carrying intervening obstacles. But the trade-off is the longer swing that a more lofted club requires to cover the same distance. As I've said, a longer swing means greater risk of in-swing faults and poor results. You have to

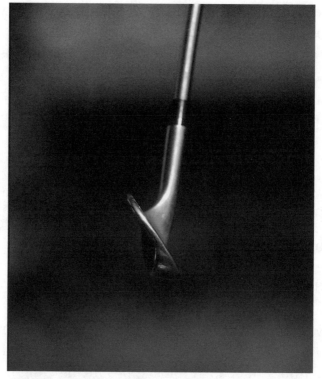

Wedges have heavy flanges to help get under the ball.

weigh your options, and make sure you're comfortable with the club you choose.

That said, you may want to use one club for all your pitch shots, as many golfers do in chipping. This creates a sense of familiarity that can be comforting when you have to face intimidating shots.

Pitching over obstacles creates tension in many players, and tension goes with touch like oil goes with water. Trust in your club selection is one good way to ease your fears and send yourself into the shot with a positive feeling.

BEST TIP: Watch Your Speed

Nothing makes a pitch swing more unpredictable than too much speed. When the hands and arms race out of sequence, they throw the swing off-track, leading to a variety of mishits. To learn speed control, practice hitting 30-yard shots with your pitching wedge using a full swing. It will feel as if you're swinging in slow motion, but don't cheat: Make sure you complete your backswing and follow-through. Gradually increase distance to 50, 70, and 100 yards. You'll gain an instant appreciation for how fast you're swinging the club.

—Craig Shankland, *GOLF Magazine*
Top 100 Teacher

Pitching Setup

Pitching can, at times, seem to be a hopeless endeavor. Consider the objectives: You want to loft the ball over obstacles and stop it quickly on the green, two things that you're probably not confident doing. As a result, you feel anxious over the ball, which leads to tense muscles, a tight grip, and quick tempo—three major obstacles in any pitch shot. What you need instead are soft hands and a little faith.

A tight grip obviously starts with the hands, but grip tension quickly spreads to the wrists, arms, and shoulders, inhibiting them from working naturally. The common by-product of this tension is unpredictable speed. If you take a stranglehold on the handle at address, you'll likely snatch the club away from the ball and make a quick swipe at it coming down.

In addition, tension reduces the range of motion in the wrists and shoulders, creating the need for the hands and arms to create hitting power (speed) on the downswing. This type of power production is unreliable, as it hinges on perfect timing of muscles in the hands and arms. It's simplest to avoid these speed issues altogether by taking a soft grip at address and keeping it soft throughout the swing, thereby de-emphasizing the hitting action of the hands and arms.

All this tension goes against our second setup essential: trust. Truth is, many amateurs doubt their ability to hit short shots high in the air. They don't trust the design of the club to help them get the ball up or their skill in putting it to use. As a result, they flip their hands quickly through the hitting area to try to create a lifting motion. That's a recipe for inconsistency.

To become a good pitcher, you have to go into every swing relaxed and confident about the outcome. Put yourself in the following setup positions every time and you'll have good reason to feel ready over the ball:

Center the ball. Position the ball midway between your heels and set your hands directly in line with the ball. With the hands just ahead of the clubface at address, the shaft leans slightly toward the target, setting up a descending angle of approach on the downswing for crisp contact.

Distribute your weight evenly. Since the pitch swing is a miniature full swing, with the same motions only performed on a reduced scale, it does feature a slight weight transfer to the back foot going back and the front foot coming down. To allow this natural weight shift in response to the

For a standard pitch, center the ball and distribute your weight evenly.

swinging motion, set your weight evenly at address, 50 percent left and 50 percent right.

Take a narrow stance.   Place your heels ten to twelve inches apart. Although your weight should transfer, you don't want to complicate the swing by moving laterally off the ball and requiring a compensating movement on the downswing to get back. With your feet close together, you'll automatically limit lateral motion to keep your balance.

Use your normal grip.   Don't grip down on the club, as you should when chipping. Gripping down lightens the club and reduces power, which, in pitching, means you'd need a longer, faster swing to compensate. Using the full length of the club also allows you to better feel the weight of the clubhead, letting it unhinge your wrists coming down and slide under the ball without any hitting action from your hands.

Set up square to slightly open.   A square stance is the simplest, as body alignment tends to follow foot alignment and a square body promotes

a straight swing path through impact. However, setting your alignment slightly open promotes another critical motion: body rotation toward the target on the downswing. This pivoting action is one of the keys to delivering the clubhead to the ball in a shallow, undercutting motion. Experiment with a square and a slightly open stance to find out which is better for you.

Aim the clubface square to slightly open.

In chipping, a square clubface is best because the swing is so short and slow that the ball simply rebounds off the clubface. But for longer, faster swings, the ball will start on a line somewhere between the direction of the swing path and the direction the clubface is pointing in at impact. If you play from a square stance, you'll tend to swing straight along the target line through impact, so square the clubface at address. If you open your stance at address, you'll tend to cut across the line from out to in through impact, so open the face to send the ball slightly to the right of the swing path. An open clubface also adds loft to the shot. There is no one best way—it comes down to what makes you comfortable and confident.

***BEST TIP:** Hoop Dreams*

Most amateurs tend to leave the ball short when pitching to an elevated green and only the top of the flagstick is visible. To produce a longer shot, they need a sensory cue that makes them hit the ball harder. I have my students envision a basketball hoop, which stands ten feet tall, in place of the flag. If they try to swish their pitch shot through the hoop, they'll have a much better chance of getting the ball to the hole.

—Dr. Richard Coop, *GOLF Magazine*
Mental Game Consultant

Pitching Swing

As strange as it may sound, pitching requires power—quite a bit of power, in fact. You might not think so, considering the soft, floating shots it produces, but the pitching swing requires a forceful motion because the power is used to send the ball as much upward as forward. The force is more under the ball at impact than behind it.

Think of what happens when you hit a pitch shot thinly. The leading edge catches the middle of the ball and sends it screaming over the green. That's because the power of the swing launches the ball forward, not upward as expected. As a result, the ball flies three or four times farther than planned—all due to misdirected power.

The good news is, you don't have to worry about directing the power during the swing; you've set it up with your club selection and address positions. You see, by using the highest lofted clubs for pitching, you're hitting the ball with a clubface that's tilted away from the target. At impact, this produces oblique contact with the ball that pushes it upward as well as forward. The higher the loft, the more oblique the contact, with the energy of the swing farther under the ball, producing a higher shot.

The setup positions just discussed likewise force the swing's energy under the ball. By distributing your weight evenly and playing the ball in the middle of your stance, you promote a slight downward blow, as compared to the sharp descent used in chipping. This more level angle of attack puts the heavy sole of the clubhead under the ball at impact, producing a higher launch angle off the clubface and more lift.

Now you need to add power. To hit a pitch shot (which travels both forward and upward) the same distance as a chip shot (which travels essentially only forward), you need a much longer, faster swing. In chipping, the swing employs a single lever, from the left shoulder to the ball; in pitching, the swing uses two levers, the left arm and the club, with a hinge at the wrist. This hinge allows you to make a longer swing and to generate the added power you need.

As you may already be piecing together, the pitch swing is really the full swing in miniature. Not only does it feature a significant wrist hinge, but the need for more power also produces a fuller body turn and even a slight weight transfer back and through. These elements, which are crucial power producers in the full swing, can be found to smaller degrees in even the shortest pitch shots. So while you may not want to *think* power when pitching, you need to generate a fair amount of it to be an effective pitcher.

Here are the keys to executing a standard pitch shot, which, with a pitching wedge, should send the ball about 30 yards—15 yards in the air and another 15 on the ground.

Check your grip pressure.   In order for the wrists to hinge freely on the backswing, the hands have to keep a light grip on the club. Try slowly

The pitching swing features a full wrist hinge.

waggling the club back and forth at address to keep the hands soft and the wrists limber and ready to perform. Keeping the club in motion makes you more aware of your grip pressure and also serves to keep the hands and wrists active and therefore less susceptible to unwanted tension.

Start the arms and shoulders together.

As with the chip shot, the arms and shoulders start back together, causing the body to pivot away from the target. It's imperative to keep your head perfectly still; any vertical or lateral head movement on the backswing has to be "undone" before impact for solid contact to occur. Feel as if you're moving around a fixed axis, with your arms swinging and your body turning as a single unit.

Hinge the clubhead up.   Almost immediately

as you swing back, start hinging the club up, pointing the toe of the clubhead to the sky. Even on a thirty-yard pitch shot, the wrists should hinge the club into nearly a 90-degree angle with the left arm. The longer swing created by this hinging action should be supported by added rotation in the shoulders and hips, even a slight weight transfer.

The shoulders turn as the arms swing the club back.

However, do not consciously shift your weight; the weight will move naturally as a result of the actions of the upper body. Your focus should be on making a smooth, unified move away from the ball.

Synchronize the downswing. To return the clubhead to the ball, simply swing everything through together, as if you were in a body cast and couldn't move any parts independently. The centrifugal force of the downswing will unhinge the wrists and pull the club into a straight line with the left arm at impact. Feel as if you're just letting the clubhead drop as you turn through with your entire body—knees, hips, chest, shoulders.

Let it go. You have to trust that you've established the necessary loft in your setup and the necessary power in your backswing; the downswing is a simple reversal of the backswing positions on the way to the finish. Too many amateurs see it as a last-ditch effort to manipulate the position or speed of the clubhead with their hands and arms. No golfer can save swings in this manner on a consistent basis.

Feel as if you're simply letting the club drop as you turn
your body through.

Finish your pivot. If your body turns smoothly through impact, you've stayed relaxed and not tried to overcontrol the shot. To monitor hand and wrist tension, think about the club rehinging into a 90-degree angle with your right arm on the follow-through, a mirror image of your left arm and the club on the backswing. At the finish, your belt buckle and chest should face the target and almost all of your weight should be on your left heel. These positions indicate that you've used the big muscles of your body, not just the quickness of your hands and arms, to deliver the club to the ball.

BEST TIP: Release Your Fears

If your fear factor is high on pitch shots, I bet your lower body isn't working properly. Fear freezes the big muscles, locking the lower body in place, and activates the small muscles in the hands and arms. That is a risky prescription for a pitch shot.

To return leg action to its proper role, start your downswing by rolling your right ankle and knee toward the target. This move helps the big muscles stay loose and perform as they should and promotes high, soft shots that clear even the most fearsome obstacles.

—Paul Trittler, *GOLF Magazine* Top 100 Teacher

Relaxed hands and wrists will rehinge the club on the follow-through.

Common Faults

Most pitching faults occur when golfers try to help the ball into the air. With little faith in the club's built-in loft or the technique just described, they think they have to manufacture extra loft to carry the ball safely onto the green. As a result, they try to lift the ball by manipulating impact. Such manipulation has many forms, but consider the three most common.

Let's start with the setup. Golfers intent on producing a lifting motion often set up "behind the ball," meaning they set more weight on their rear foot, tilt their spine away from the target, and play the ball up toward their front foot. From there, they feel as if they can undercut the ball and thereby increase the height of the shot.

Other golfers set up okay, but then try to create these behind-the-ball positions during the swing. They shift to their rear foot on the backswing and stay there, swinging the clubhead up at the ball. The typical result in both cases is poor contact, since moving the ball up or moving the body back puts the bottom of the swing arc behind the ball. The club either bottoms out in the ground before it reaches the ball or catches it on the upswing. They're either chunking it or skulling it.

Another in-swing fault is "the scoop," or a premature unhinging of the right wrist in an attempt to lift the ball by flipping the hands. Although good players will sometimes use this unhinging motion to maximize loft, it's an ill-advised method for the middle to high handicapper, as it requires a keen feel for what the clubhead is doing. In effect, you're creating the bottom of the swing arc with your hands and wrists. If you don't catch the ball perfectly, the resulting shot will be either fat or thin.

Players who try to manufacture extra loft need to resign themselves to one simple truth: You can hit down on the ball and still hit a high shot. In fact, you should always make a slight downward strike on greenside shots to ensure flush contact; the wedges have plenty of

"This Is Not a Toy"

There's a serious problem spreading through the amateur ranks: lob-wedge dependence. More and more amateurs are grabbing their lob wedge for all sorts of greenside shots, instead of reserving it for when they really need extra height. Remember, the higher the shot, the longer the swing must be to cover any given distance; this sends the risk factor through the roof. Lob wedges should come with a warning label: "This is not a toy." For some, the novelty soon wears off, but too many have reinvented their short game around this modern-day weapon. Loft should inspire caution, not comfort.

"Scooping" through impact is a common pitching fault.

loft to launch the ball into the air. That's easy to say, but to become a believer you have to learn for yourself that "down means up," and then have the courage to trust it when you're standing over the ball.

Pitching Variations

Now that I've taken such pains to caution you against the perils of pitching, let's look at a few descendants of the pitch shot that demand even more prudence in planning and execution. They come in two forms: shots where the stance or lie of the ball is unusual and shots requiring greater height or distance than the standard pitch provides. Practice them before you put them in your bag; in time, they'll save you shots, if you use them wisely.

The Lob Shot

When you're asked to carry the ball over bunkers or deep rough and stop it quickly on the green, you need a shot that flies almost straight up in the air and dribbles to a stop after landing. This is com-

For a lob shot, hinge the club up abruptly.

monly referred to as the lob shot, and anyone who's tried it knows it takes some chutzpah.

First, take your most lofted wedge, preferably a lob wedge, although a sand wedge will do. However, do not use a sand wedge with a lot of "bounce," a design characteristic caused by the trailing edge of the sole being lower than the leading edge. This feature prevents the clubhead from digging on contact; it's great in the sand, but when used anywhere else can cause the clubhead to ricochet off the ground and into the ball.

To execute the lob shot, open your stance about 30 degrees and play the ball slightly ahead of center, with your weight evenly distributed. Whether you're using a sand or lob wedge, point the leading edge of the clubface at the target. From there, make a long, slow swing, hinging your wrists immediately on the backswing and rehinging them immediately after impact. You want to make a three-quarter swing at half-speed, sliding the clubface under the ball and continuing into the finish. As you might imagine, this is not the type of shot that can be used effectively with little practice. Work on it before you try it during an actual round.

> ### BEST TIP: Right for Height
>
> The lob shot takes some getting used to, as the swing is long but the shot is short. To generate a long enough swing and the necessary shallow approach into impact, try to feel an underarm throwing motion with the right arm. Take practice swings (then hit balls) with your left hand off the club and let your right arm create the wide arc and shallow approach necessary to slip the leading edge under the ball.
>
> —Dick Harmon, *GOLF Magazine*
> Top 100 Teacher

The Half-Wedge

Hitting a wedge half of its full distance is a tricky proposition for most. It catches the golfer between full-swing mode and short-game mode, with the result often being uncertainty and poor execution. The best way to deal with this shot is to steer clear of situations where you would need it: Half-wedges often stem from poor decisions, such as hitting a layup too far or punching out of trouble to an awkward distance. In short, don't put yourself in half-wedge territory.

But despite your best planning efforts, you'll still come across this shot now and then. When you do, your main objective should be to keep the arms and

---

BEST TIP: *Steady as She Goes*

On half-wedge shots, it's vital that the body's center of gravity remain stable. To ingrain stability, practice with a golf ball wedged under the outside of each foot. The balls prohibit the knees and hips from sliding laterally and force the muscles in the hips, back, and shoulders to turn and support the swinging motion.

—Kent Cayce, *GOLF Magazine* Top 100 Teacher

body linked throughout the entire motion. Many golfers try to take power off the swing by restricting body turn or decelerating the club on the downswing. These are unreliable ways of controlling distance; the former causes excess tension, the latter puts the hands in control.

To execute the half-wedge, start by taking a narrow stance, with your heels twelve to fifteen inches apart, and setting the ball in the middle. Then swing the club halfway back, the shaft reaching vertical, and keep your body centered. From there, swing the club and turn the body through together, keeping your left wrist firm through impact and letting the shaft reach vertical on the follow-through. With some practice, this shot will not be quite so intimidating.

Hilly Lies

Approach shots that miss the green often find uneven terrain, especially with all the greenside mounding and bunkering found on modern-day courses. That's why it's crucial to know how to adjust your standard pitching technique to accommodate uphill, downhill, and sidehill lies.

When pitching from hilly lies, swing with the slope, not into it.

When pitching uphill or downhill, it's easy to mishit the ball; you'll tend to hit fat shots going uphill and thin shots going downhill, because gravity pulls your body in the direction of the slope during the swing. To counter this, set more weight on your uphill foot at address and try to keep it there throughout the swing. Also, try to align your shoulders parallel to the angle of the ground and focus on swinging with the slope, not into it.

For sidehill lies, your main objective must be to make contact without the toe or heel of the club-head catching the ground first. When the ball lies above your feet, the toe will tend to hit the ground first; when the ball lies below, the heel is likely to catch. To encourage solid contact, make sure you set the sole of your wedge flush to the ground at address. If the ball is above your feet, stand more upright and make a more around-the-body swing; if the ball is below your feet, bend your knees more and make a more up-and-down motion.

Deep Rough

There are times when you need the height of a pitch shot, but the lie is too thick to allow clean contact using the standard pitching technique. We all know that feeling of hopelessness when we catch a clump of heavy rough before the ball and the clubhead loses its will to go on.

The best option here is a modified pitch shot—something between a chip and a pitch. You need the steeper angle into the ball that a chip features to catch it cleanly, but you also need the higher loft and stopping power of a pitch shot. So, take what you need from each.

Using your sand or lob wedge, play the ball back toward your right instep and push your hands

To pitch from thick grass, move the ball back and make a steep swing.

ahead. With your weight favoring your left side, hinge the clubhead up quickly and then drop it back down to the ball. Don't worry about making a follow-through; your focus should be making good contact. The ball should pop out on a trajectory higher than a chip but lower than a pitch. That's how you handle the thick stuff.

Sand Play

Let's get something straight: Most amateurs are pa-
thetic in the sand—and they know it. You may
think you're a decent chipper; maybe you can even
pitch the ball with a fair bit of confidence. But if
you're like most golfers, you'd rather find your ball
buried in six-inch rough than staring at you from a
greenside bunker.

The simple truth is that most poor bunker play
stems from a lack of understanding of what needs to
happen at impact. You don't have to dig halfway to
China to blast the ball out. In fact, the deeper you try
to dig the better your chances of taking too much
sand and—dare I say—leaving it in the bunker. The
only thing worse than not getting out of the sand the
first time is having the chance to do it over again.

So why do the pros look so darned comfortable in the sand? Because they know two advantages that sand shots have over other greenside shots: predictability and forgiveness. First, the pros know sand is a fairly predictable playing surface from one shot to the next, in terms of both firmness and depth. Assuming your ball is sitting on top of the sand, you know what lies underneath it. That's where you're guessing with other lies; even in seemingly good lies in the grass, you never know how firm it is underneath. You don't have that uncertainty when you're in the sand.

The second reason pros like sand is that it is forgiving; it leaves room for error. Since your clubface never comes in contact with the ball on bunker shots, solid contact—perhaps your biggest fear in other greenside shots—is simply not an issue. In fact, with the right swing, you can enter the sand an inch or so closer to or farther from the ball than you planned and still produce a decent shot. Where else can you say that around the green?

So before you conclude that you'll never be much of a bunker player, read through the instruction that follows. It's a lot simpler than you may think, and could easily become a strength in your game. Maybe you'll start wishing for bunker shots, like the pros sometimes do—or at least not feel as if you're doomed when your ball ends up on the beach.

How to Plan a Bunker Shot

Most golfers climb into bunkers with a fair amount of mental baggage. Each can tell you horror stories of disaster holes or career rounds ended in the sand. And every one of us can commiserate. But those are

> ### No Choking
>
> For most golfers, sand means tension. And the first place tension rears its ugly head is in the grip, where the fingers strangle the handle and send pressure up the arms and into the body. The usual result is a fast, jerky swing and inconsistent shots. To nip tension in the bud, "milk" the handle at address, exerting and releasing pressure with your fingers. Don't take the club back until your grip feels soft. Only then are you ready to go.

harmful thoughts as you step up to a bunker shot. You need a clear, confident approach and a simple plan of attack.

First, be thankful that the two major decisions you usually have to make next to the green—shot selection and club selection—are no-brainers in the sand. The basic bunker technique I'm about to discuss works for most greenside sand shots, and the sand wedge should be your weapon of choice in

A simple plan and positive visualization are crucial in bunker play.

A club has "bounce" if the trailing edge of the sole is lower than the leading edge.

virtually every situation. (Due to its "bounce" feature, the sand wedge slides through the sand instead of digging.) So, there are two fewer things to think about. And you thought this was hard?

Your first order of business, assuming you have a decent lie, is deciding where you want to hit the shot. This may sound obvious, but you don't always want to play directly to the hole. For instance, if you're staring at the tallest part of the bunker lip or you have deep trouble directly behind the hole, you may want to look for a safer route. That decision hinges on how much confidence you have in your sand game. But for most players, it's better to be thinking about getting on the green, not getting to the hole.

Once you know where you're going, pick a landing area. It may be difficult to zero in on a specific spot, but figure out the general area where you want the ball to touch down. This gives you something positive to focus on, rather than bad memories or the opportunity for disaster that the shot presents. Simply pick your shot, then your spot, and keep your thoughts focused and positive.

Although we're about to look at setup and swing mechanics, bunker play is largely about feel. Swinging through the sand produces a much different sensation than hitting the ball directly; you should pre-sense how you want your body and the club to feel as you prepare to hit the shot. Focus less on the technique of the swing and more on how the club should move through the impact area. As you become a better bunker player, you'll rely almost totally on your instincts in the sand.

One last point on preparation: Check your tension level. Negative thoughts and fear cause tension, which tightens the grip and quickens the swing. Take a few deep breaths and shake out your hands. And remember, try to draw on the good experiences you've had, not the heartbreakers.

Bunker Setup

First, realize that the prevailing technique used in bunker play has changed. Traditional instruction says the bunker swing is a steep, out-to-in swipe that slices across the line, digging under the ball and popping it out of the sand. Today, most instructors teach a shallower swing that slides the club-

---

BEST TIP: *Predictable Roll*

Tour pros rarely use the traditional out-to-in swing for bunker shots. We know it imparts a lot of left-to-right sidespin on the ball, which can be difficult to plan for on the landing. Instead, we prefer a more normal swing path, the clubhead cutting a swath in the sand that points to the target. Picture a rectangle in the sand with the ball in the middle and make a steep swing back and through, trying to slice the entire rectangle out of the sand. A straight swing will produce a straight roll.

—Curtis Strange, two-time
U.S. Open Champion

---

head just under the surface of the sand and clips the ball off the top. This new method has proven to be more effective and more forgiving.

As a result of this change in thinking, the traditional bunker setup has also undergone an overhaul. The old stance was dramatically open, with the feet sunk deep in the sand, to promote a backswing to the outside and a steep, explosive descent into the ball. The new setup is designed to let you move the clubhead in a normal swing arc, from the inside coming down and back to the inside on the follow-through. This path creates a shallower approach to the ball and a longer, thinner cut in the sand.

The following setup keys will put you in position to execute the modern bunker shot.

Open the clubface. This exposes the bounce on the bottom of the sole and adds loft to the clubface. However, you should open the face before you step into the bunker: With your left hand on the grip, rotate the club clockwise about 20 degrees with your right hand and then take your normal grip with both hands. If you merely turn the clubface open at address, without changing your hand positions, you haven't really opened the clubface at all.

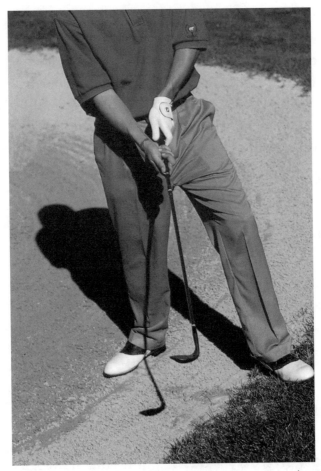

Before you enter the sand, rotate the face open, then take your grip.

Play the ball forward.   Since you actually want to make fat contact, touching down in the sand first, position the ball about an inch in front of the center of your stance. Let your arms hang naturally; your hands should be slightly behind the ball at address, the shaft tilting neither toward nor away from the target. This promotes a fairly level swipe through the sand, with the ball in the middle of your sand divot.

Take a wider stance.   Even if you dig your feet in, your stance in a bunker is never rock-solid due to the shifting nature of the sand. To create a steady base, spread your feet apart so your insteps are at hip-width. You still won't be able to transfer much weight or move laterally off the ball, which will do wonders for your consistency. Your objective is to make a smooth, accelerating swing while staying in perfect balance.

Align slightly open.   Shift your stance, as well as your knees, hips, and shoulders, about 20 degrees open to the target. This open position presets a full rotation of the body through the shot, a move that many amateurs fail to make in the sand. Once your

For a standard shot, play the ball just ahead of center.

feet are positioned, twist them down into the sand about an inch, which lowers your entire body and therefore the bottom of the swing arc. Remember, you want the swing to bottom out in the sand under the ball, not at ball level.

Aim an inch behind the ball. You actually want to contact the sand about two or three inches behind the ball, but if you aim the leading edge about an inch behind it, the bounce factor of your sand wedge will cause the trailing edge to enter the sand first. But try not to get too stuck on this aiming point: If you make it the focus of the entire swing, you'll probably fail to swing the clubhead through the sand—a common amateur mistake.

BEST TIP: Dial the Face

Control the depth of your divot holes in the sand by increasing or decreasing the angle of the flange—the clubhead's protruding sole. The more you open the clubface—also known as "dialing the face"—the greater the angle of the flange, which prevents you from digging too deep in the sand. I like to play most of my bunker shots with the leading edge pointing toward 1:30 or 2 o'clock. This shallows out the divot and adds loft and spin to the shot.

—Phil Rodgers, *GOLF Magazine*
Top 100 Teacher

Bunker Swing

Many golfers feel as if they have to manufacture a totally different swing when they step into the sand. They try to make a steep, out-to-in motion that they use nowhere else on the golf course. This is a mistake.

Truth is, anyone who can make a simple pitch swing can hit a good bunker shot—and that means any golfer. The motion is essentially the same: Swing the club and turn the body in one motion, then move everything through together. The fact that you're hitting sand instead of a golf ball should not affect the swing; the only difference is that the bunker swing needs to be longer and faster to hit the ball the same distance as a normal pitch shot. Practice will tell you how far your standard bunker shot travels compared to your standard pitch.

Hank Johnson, one of *GOLF Magazine*'s Top 100 Teachers, discusses this relationship in his book *How to Win the Three Games of Golf*: "I usually count on a 3-to-1 ratio. A swing that would hit a standard pitch 30 yards would hit a bunker shot 10 yards. A stroke that would send a standard pitch 60 yards would result in a 20-yard bunker shot."

Relating your bunker swing to your pitching swing should be helpful: It's a move away from the old out-to-in method, and should help dispel the mystique of sand play by linking it to something with which you're more comfortable.

Here are the swing keys for a standard greenside bunker shot:

Hover the clubhead. Be thankful for the rule that prohibits you from grounding your clubhead in the sand. By having to support the weight of the club at address, you sustain a constant grip pressure, which promotes a smooth, unhurried takeaway. Given the tension that most golfers feel in the sand, it's also a good idea to waggle the clubhead back and forth or up and down to quiet stress in the hands and arms.

Start the arms and shoulders together.
Make a one-piece takeaway, turning your shoulders as your arms swing the club on a slightly inside path. Let the wrists hinge the club upward, an action that will happen naturally provided your grip is light and your wrists are supple. Think of the lower body as the base of the

swing: The hips and legs should support the actions of the arms and torso, responding to motion, not creating motion.

Make a three-quarter backswing.

Lengthening your backswing is the best way to promote more clubhead speed coming down so you can power through the sand. At the top, your wrists should be fully hinged, the club at a right angle to your left arm, and your hands should be at about shoulder height. Also, make a three-quarter body turn away from the ball, with your back almost to the target and your left shoulder nearly under your chin. These backswing positions set up a proper move into impact.

Turn and swing through impact.

From the top, turn your body and swing your arms down in one synchronized movement. Provided your arms don't rush out in front, the club will track back down to the ball on an inside path, producing a shallow entry into the sand and a long, thin divot. The old out-to-in technique produces bomb craters because the downswing is a steep motion controlled mainly by the arms. Today's method features more

Make a three-quarter backswing with a full wrist hinge.

Cut a shallow divot and keep the clubhead moving.

body rotation back and through, which shallows out the swing and helps the clubhead slip through the sand, rather than slam into it.

Continue to a three-quarter finish. The
shallower swing arc allows you to swing through

At the finish, the chest should be turned to the target.

the sand with less resistance and therefore achieve a fuller finish. Your clubhead should touch down two to three inches behind the ball and slide underneath it. As a result, the ball will fly out on a pillow of sand without ever making contact with the clubface. Impact should be a muffled "thump," like the sound of beating out an old rug. At the finish, your chest should face the target, indicating full body rotation on the downswing.

BEST TIP: How to Vary Distance

Many amateurs have trouble varying distance on bunker shots. Part of the problem is how they finish: They swing into a full follow-through regardless of the shot at hand. As a rule, the length of the follow-through should correspond to the length of the shot. A short shot needs a short follow-through, and a long shot needs a long follow-through. You wouldn't finish with the club up over your shoulder on a short pitch shot; so don't do it for a short bunker shot either. Match your finish to the shot you need.

—Martin Hall, *GOLF Magazine*
Master Teaching Professional

Common Faults

Most poor bunker shots result from one of two problems: fear or misunderstanding. The fear we can take care of with positive experiences, which come from understanding what you have to do to produce the desired results. It's as simple as that: Fix your technique, hit some effective shots, and the fear should shrink away.

That leaves us with grooving the right technique. To begin with, try to erase from your mind the image of a steep blast out of the sand, since that is the biggest technique fault among amateurs. If you try to make a steep swing, you'll instinctively freeze your body and swing the club up and down with only your hands and arms. The result is a fast, rigid lash—a move you see from virtually every poor bunker player.

Such a move can produce either fat or thin shots, often in alternating fashion. You see, a steep swing requires great precision, as the clubhead has to enter the sand very close to the ball to produce an acceptable shot. If a steep swing enters the sand a little too far behind the ball, the clubhead will lose too much momentum and yield a fat shot; if it enters too close, the result is the dreaded skulled shot.

Most golfers try to dig the ball out with a steep swing.

Simply put, a steep swing has to be a precise swing, and that's a lot to ask in an intimidating situation.

Instead, envision a shallow cut through the sand. To shallow out an overly steep swing, you need to add body rotation. Focus on the takeaway: Start the

Spinning from the Sand

To increase backspin on bunker shots, you have to swing the club faster through the bottom of the swing arc, sliding the clubface on a shallow angle through the sand. Think of it as knocking the legs out from under the ball. Visualize the clubhead passing under the ball and beating it out on the other side. To produce this fast cutting action, lay the clubface wide open at address and focus on fast body rotation back and through.

club back with the hands, arms, and shoulders moving as a single unit, the clubhead sweeping slightly to the inside and low to the ground. Provided you don't yank the club down from the top, the downswing will return on the same path and skim through the sand, pushing the ball up and out. A good swing thought to increase body rotation is "Turn your back to the target on the backswing, then turn your chest to the target on the through-swing." Don't get stuck thinking about impact; concentrate on the overall swing motion.

Bunker-Shot Variations

The Long Bunker Shot

When you're in the sand but need more than the standard 10- to 15-yard bunker shot, you need to transfer more energy to the ball at impact. To do this, many amateurs either swing harder or try to make contact closer to the ball. Problem is, hard swings mean wild swings, and closing the gap between the clubface and the ball at impact requires too much precision to be reliable.

There is a better option. First, put away your sand wedge, and opt for a pitching wedge or 9-iron—even an 8- or 7-iron for a longer shot. These clubs have more upright faces, which apply more forward propulsion and less upward propulsion as they enter the sand. Use the same technique described above, except square the stance and the clubface to produce more direct impact, and you'll hit a shot that comes out lower and hotter and rolls after landing.

The Buried Lie

Always a gruesome discovery, the buried bunker lie strikes fear in even the most experienced golfers. Knowing that the objective of a bunker shot is to swing the clubface under the ball, golfers typically try to pound down on buried lies, hoping that extra power will create deeper penetration into the sand. Sometimes this works, sometimes it doesn't.

For longer bunker shots, change clubs, not technique.

To get the ball up and out of a buried lie, you need the clubface to dig, not bounce. Play the ball farther back in your stance, just behind center, and push your hands slightly ahead—both promote more of a digging motion. Also, place a little more weight on your left foot and set the clubface square or even slightly closed. From there, just make your normal bunker swing; the setup changes will produce a steeper swing that helps the clubface cut through the sand and move under the ball. Expect a lower trajectory and minimal backspin.

BEST TIP: *Facing the Buried Lie*

To extricate a ball buried in a bunker, the clubhead must approach at a steep angle and dig deep into the sand. As a result, the hosel that connects the clubhead to the shaft plows into the sand just as the clubface does. In normal bunker shots, only the clubface compacts sand, and the ball flies out in the direction in which the clubface is aimed. With buried lies, the hosel also compacts sand, pushing it to the right. To compensate for this, aim the clubface farther to the left at address.

—David Feherty, television commentator and former Ryder Cup player

From a buried lie, play the ball back and lean left to promote a digging action.

From Wet Sand

You may think playing from wet sand should be much like playing from a buried lie, since both situations present the problem of getting under the ball. However, wet sand is very firm and difficult to penetrate. You need to adjust your approach.

When the sand is wet, use a wedge with as little bounce as possible, preferably a lob wedge, as you want to minimize the ricochet effect off the firm sand. Open both your clubface and your stance about 30 degrees, and play the ball off your left instep. Make your normal bunker swing, entering the sand about an inch farther behind the ball, which gives the clubface more time to dig into the firmer surface. Make sure you hold the clubface open through impact so that more of the clubhead can slide under the ball.

You may have to swing a little harder to keep the clubhead moving through the packed sand, but try to achieve at least a half-length finish, as this mindset will ensure an accelerating motion through impact. Again, expect a lower ball flight and reduced backspin.

Specialty Shots

To borrow a phrase from Wall Street, an efficient short game is grounded in risk management. Smart golfers rarely play a risky shot when a safer one can produce similar results. This may seem like routine decision-making, but there are legions of golfers out there who overlook the risks involved in greenside shots, who pitch the ball when they could chip it or play the sky-high lob at every opportunity. These folks will never realize their potential as golfers.

This is not to suggest that every time a golfer strays from standard chipping, pitching, or bunker technique that he is taking unnecessary risk. Fact is, a risky shot in some circumstances is a smart play in others. For instance, the long swing required to hit a lob shot is risky, but in some cases

---

BEST TIP: *Ultrahigh Flop Shot*

When there is very little green to work with or a tall obstacle, such as a high bunker lip, between you and the hole, you need a high shot that stops immediately. Using a sand or lob wedge, place the ball off the middle of your front foot, open the clubface 30 to 40 degrees, and set your hands a couple of inches behind the ball. On the backswing, make a cupping action with the left wrist, arching the back of the left hand toward the forearm, to open the clubface even more. Imagine a pile of sand on the clubface at address; during the takeaway, rotate the clubface open so the sand dumps on the ground behind you. Make a full backswing, then swing the clubhead down along the target line. The result will be a very high, soft-landing shot.

—Lee Janzen, two-time U.S. Open Champion

---

it's safer than the standard pitch shot. Say a small green requires that you drop a pitch on the front fringe to avoid rolling over. In this case, the higher-flying lob gives you more room for error on the landing. It's a riskier swing but a safer shot.

Aside from the shot variations I've already discussed, there are times when you're really forced to

BEST TIP: To loft the ball high and stop it quickly, open the clubface at address and rotate it more open during the backswing.

think "outside the box" in greenside situations. From one shot to the next, your lie can go from firm to soft, the grass from thick to thin, and your path to the hole from unimpeded to seemingly impassable. Decide right now to accept that: You cannot control where your ball goes after you hit it, and you'll never play a good shot dwelling on what you perceive as a bad break. When your ball finds a tricky situation, think of it as a chance to be creative and have some fun.

Does this mean throw caution to the wind? Hardly. The shots we're about to look at are actually safer plays than the standard greenside shots we've been discussing—provided the situation calls for them. That's the key: You have to decide between a more familiar shot and a more inventive one designed for very specific situations. Are the circumstances strong enough to warrant a major departure in technique? Remember, your confidence in the shot will show in your execution.

So, keep that decision process in mind as you read through the specialty shots that follow. First, make sure the circumstances at hand demand the shot you want to play, then check your comfort level. If one of the standard greenside shots is a viable option, use it; if you think a specialty shot is the way to go, commit to it and enjoy being creative.

The Bellied Wedge

The Situation:

Your ball has run through the fringe and nestled up against the edge of the rough. Although the ball actually lies on closely mown grass, where you'd typically putt or chip, the long grass behind the ball will grab the clubhead if you use a normal putting or chipping motion. You need a swing that will slide the clubhead through the grass without it getting stuck.

The Shot:

All you need to play from this precarious situation are a sand wedge and a little common sense. First, realize that the thick, heavy sole of a sand wedge slides through long grass fairly easily, provided it doesn't sink too deep. Since you only have to nudge the ball forward and get it rolling, the best way to handle this lie is to play an intentional thin shot, contacting the middle of the ball with the leading edge of the clubface.

To do this, set up as you normally would for a putt—ball centered, hands slightly ahead of the

With the ball up against the collar, try "The Bellied Wedge."

clubhead, eyes over the ball—except grip down about an inch on the handle. If you stay in your normal putting posture, choking down should raise the clubhead up about an inch off the ground. Then, simply line up the leading edge with the ball's equator and make a straight-back, straight-through sweep, like a putting stroke, keeping your head and lower body perfectly still. The ball will skip forward and roll smoothly.

The Wood Chip

The Situation:

Again, you've narrowly missed the green, but this time you find yourself in thick grass just off the fringe. A standard chip shot could do the job, but it would be difficult to catch the ball cleanly in the heavy grass without dropping the clubhead almost directly on top of the ball, which can make the shot very unpredictable.

The Shot:

Similar to the bottom of a sand wedge, the rounded head of a fairway wood glides through long grass more easily than an iron head. In fact, the molded bottoms of most fairway woods help the clubhead slide instead of dig, parting grass as it goes and promoting a clean hit. This sliding action comes in handy on greenside shots, provided you

A fairway wood can be an effective chipping club.

don't need to carry the ball, as these clubs feature minimal loft.

The first step in executing a fairway-wood chip is choking down to the bottom of the grip to wield better control over the long shaft. Then take your normal pitching setup—ball centered, hands slightly ahead of the ball, weight evenly distributed—and make a simple pendulum motion with the arms and shoulders, letting the clubhead slide through the grass. You may trap some grass between the clubface and the ball, but the grass will not grab the wood head like it does an iron. Get used to this shot on the practice green before trying it on the course.

The Bunker Putt

The Situation:

Chasing a hole cut close to a side bunker, you get too cute with your approach shot and find the sand. Now you face a ticklish little shot with just a few paces of green between you and the hole. Your standard bunker shot will get you out of the sand but will release to the far side of the green. In this

---

Get a Good Leave

As golf architect Robert Trent Jones Jr. notes in his book *Golf By Design,* "like pool, golf is primarily a game of position ... The key is to get a good 'leave,' or an ideal position for the next shot." On greenside plays, this means leaving yourself with a makable putt, or at least an easy two-putt. If the greens are fast or severely sloped, you'd sometimes rather be ten feet below the hole than five feet above it. Point is, your target doesn't always have to be the hole; be aware of areas you want to avoid.

situation, consider putting the ball, instead of trying to finesse a bunker shot.

The Shot:

For the bunker putt to be a smart play, several conditions first need to be satisfied. To begin with, the sand must be firm and smooth, and your ball must be sitting up cleanly in a flat area. Next, the bunker lip must be flat enough so the ball doesn't jump straight up as it rolls over it. Finally, the grass between the bunker and the putting surface must be dry and fairly short to allow the ball to bounce through it.

If these conditions are met, this simple shot can be very effective. The key to executing it correctly is contacting the ball at the exact bottom of the swing arc to produce a forward skipping action through the sand. If you make a downward strike, you'll drive the ball into the sand; if you make contact on the upswing, you'll hit the ball weakly and leave it short.

Take your normal putting stance and play the ball precisely between your heels. Do not dig your feet into the sand—you want a level stroke into the back of the ball without contacting the sand. As for

Putting from the sand requires a very still body.

the stroke itself, think of it as a long lag putt. You may have to let your wrists hinge slightly going back to create a long enough backswing, but try to keep your head and lower body very quiet. Then, swing the putterhead through the ball aggressively, never letting it touch the sand.

The Banker

The Situation:

Your approach to an elevated green sails wide and your ball trickles down to the base of the green's bank. You can see only the top of the flagstick, which is unsettling in itself, and you feel like you need to loft the ball up in the air and land it perfectly on the near fringe. But given the flat lie and the precise landing required, the high pitch is a low-percentage play.

The Shot:

Hitting the ball into the bank and bouncing it onto the green may be your best option, provided the grass on the bank is not so thick as to smother the ball on contact. If you feel confident that the ball will bounce up the hill, take a middle to short iron, whatever will put the first bounce about two thirds of the way up the hill, and make a short punch swing. Play the ball back in your stance and set your weight left to promote clean contact.

When you play this shot, you may be fighting your instincts in two areas. First, you probably have

Hitting into the slope can be smarter than going over it.

to hit the ball about twice as hard as you think, as the first bounce into the slope is like hitting a wall; it takes a tremendous amount of energy off the shot. Second, you're so accustomed to using a wedge for greenside shots, you'll probably pick a club with too much loft and risk clearing the hill instead of bouncing into it. Keep these tendencies in mind and practice this shot into hills of varying grades to develop a feel for when and how to use it.

BEST TIP: *The Chop Shot*

When your ball finds shin-high rough around the green, you need a shot that will power through the grass and dig it out; that's "the chop shot." Play the ball off your back foot and lean toward the target, keeping your weight there throughout the swing. Swing the club back abruptly, cocking the wrists fully, and deliver a descending blow, cutting the grass behind the ball on the approach. Try to take a divot in front of the ball and strive to keep the club moving through the grass at least two feet past impact.

—Dave Pelz, *GOLF Magazine* Technical and
Short Game Consultant

The Grassy Blast

The Situation:

At first glance, this shot doesn't look so bad: your ball lies in moderate rough only 15 or 20 feet off the fringe, with plenty of green to work with. A standard pitch should do the trick, right? Not so quick. On more careful examination, you see the grass, although not long, is very dense, surrounding the ball like a bird's nest (called a "nesty lie"). Your normal pitch swing will trap too much grass between the clubface and the ball, making contact and distance unpredictable. In this case, you have to give in to the lie; you simply cannot manufacture clean contact.

The Shot:

The best way to handle a nesty lie is to blast out of it as if you were hitting a bunker shot. Your weapon of choice should be one of the wedges: a sand wedge with bounce if the ball is sitting up; a lob or pitching wedge if the clubface needs to dig to accommodate a deeper lie.

From a nesty lie, play the ball forward and hit it like a bunker shot.

At address, play the ball two inches ahead of center, open the clubface, and aim about an inch behind the ball. Then make a half-swing, letting the wrists hinge the club back to vertical and through to vertical, trying to slide the clubface under the ball. Like in a bunker, the clubface never actually hits the ball, and therefore you need a more forceful swing than you might expect.

The ball will come out high and soft, with minimal backspin, due to the cushioned impact provided by the thick grass. Be forewarned: It takes some guts to hit this shot as hard as you have to, especially if the grass is growing away from the target, which will further kill the clubhead's momentum on contact. However, once you get comfortable with it, this shot can be a major stroke-saver.

The Hook Chip

The Situation:

You've come up just short of the green and the hole is cut way in the back. With only a few yards of fairway and all that green to cover, you could easily play a standard chip with a mid-iron, bouncing the ball onto the front edge and letting it roll the rest of the way. However, the longer irons can be unwieldy for chipping and choking down for control throws off the balance of the club and can lead to sloppy execution.

The Shot:

A better bet is to play the hook chip. Essentially, this is a standard chip shot, except with right-to-left sidespin, which promotes added roll. Using your 7- or 8-iron, play the ball off your right instep and push your hands ahead. Close the clubface slightly at address and swing the clubhead in to out

"The Hook Chip" runs hard for back hole locations.

through impact, just as you would to play a hook with your full swing.

This mini-hook will come off with more running power because the closed clubface creates the effect of a less-lofted club through impact without the awkwardness of the longer shaft. This shot is particularly useful when chipping to a top tier, since the ball needs extra forward momentum to climb uphill. In effect, you're hitting a shot that would normally require a longer swing or a longer club just by imparting hook spin on the ball.

BEST TIP: *The Low Roller*

When your ball is sitting up in grass just off the green, the low roller is an effective option that presents minimal risk. First, select the lowest lofted club you can use and still land the shot on the putting surface. Set up very close to the ball, with the club up on its toe and the ball off your right instep. Bend both elbows slightly to promote a level, sweeping swing. From there, make a simple putting-type motion with the arms and shoulders. The ball will skip forward with virtually no backspin and roll to the hole.

—Jerry Mowlds, *GOLF Magazine* Top 100 Teacher

The Trap Shot

The Situation:

Your ball has come to rest on a severe upslope to the green. The lie itself is good, but you can't possibly set up the way you're supposed to for uphill lies, primarily by aligning your shoulders parallel to the slope. If you try, you'll risk toppling down the hill during the swing. Instead, you need to find a way to hit the ball while leaning into the slope so you can keep your balance.

The Shot:

No matter how determined you are, if you start to lose your balance during the swing, your body will instinctively try to save itself from falling; as a result, shot execution takes a back seat. That said, the key to handling this situation is to find firm footing and maintain it throughout the swing.

Start by selecting one of your wedges and taking a wide stance, leaning your weight into the hill like a mountain climber balancing between steps. Play the ball off your front instep and choke down to the shaft to make up for being closer to the ball. From

On severe upslopes, try to trap the ball against the ground.

there, make an abbreviated backswing and simply try to trap the back of the ball against the hill. The upslope will provide all the loft you need; concentrate on making clean contact with the back of the ball and keeping your balance.

The Half-Grass, Half-Sand Shot

The Situation:

Around the edges of bunkers, you often find sandy areas with grass growing through them—you're not really in the bunker, but you're not in the grass either. You will find it almost impossible to judge what the ground is like underneath the ball, thereby making it extremely difficult to select the appropriate shot. If you play a pitch shot and the lie turns out to be soft, you'll have to pick it perfectly, or else risk chunking it. If you try a bunker blast and the ground is firm, you'll launch your ball over the green.

The Shot:

Don't be a hero. It's not often you find one of these lies, which means you're never really comfortable standing over one. This is not the time to have visions of floating the ball to the pin and stopping it on a dime. Instead, your objective here should be to get the ball somewhere on the dance floor. Unless you have a good feel for the firmness of the lie—remember, if you're not in the bunker, you can

Play the ball back and chip it from half-grass, half-sand lies.

take practice divots—play a standard chip to the nearest spot on the green.

The uncertainty of the lie makes it imperative to hit the ball first. To ensure that you do, play the ball off your back instep and settle more weight over your front foot. Using as little loft as possible, make a simple arms-and-shoulders swing, clipping the ball off its perch and landing it on the closest edge of the putting surface. Resist the temptation of playing a riskier shot, trying to guess how the ball will come out; a little discipline and a safe play will at least keep you in the hole.

BEST TIP: Ball in Shallow Water

Hitting a ball out of water is not as unpredictable as you might think; in fact, it's a lot like hitting a greenside bunker shot. As in bunker play, the key is the setup, positioning both the ball (in your stance) and face alignment so the club will cut into the water about as deep as the bottom of the ball. Then you make an aggressive swing and continue into a full finish. Here are the adjustments to make depending on how deep the ball lies:

1. Ball mostly above the surface: clubface wide open, ball off left heel.

2. Ball one half to two thirds below surface: clubface partially open, ball between left heel and stance center.

3. Ball almost or completely below the surface: clubface square to slightly closed, ball in center to slightly behind.

—Dave Pelz, *GOLF Magazine* Technical and Short Game Consultant

Practice

Golfers typically practice for one of two reasons: They want to hit the ball more consistently, or they want to shoot lower scores. To meet the first goal, they go to the driving range and hit balls until they can't feel their hands. For the second, they go to the practice putting green, because putting is the most obvious culprit in high scores.

As a result of such practice habits, most golfers have grossly underdeveloped skills when it comes to greenside play. For instance, say you're a poor bunker player but you never hit a sand shot outside of an actual round. If you play twenty rounds a year and hit into five bunkers a round, you only hit 100 bunker shots during the course of an entire golf season. How can you expect to get any better, especially when every shot is a hit-and-hope experience?

Point is, you simply have to practice; there is no other way to develop your talents and gain confidence around the greens. But short-game practice can be much more interesting than working on your putting or your full swing. Think about it: You can play all sorts of different shots with different swings, using your imagination and playing games and competitions against yourself or a friend. The variety is as limitless as the short game itself. Enjoy the process and watch your scores start to drop.

BEST TIP: *Height Makes Right*

In the short game, trajectory is the key to controlling the total distance and the flight-to-roll ratio of the shot. I create trajectory mostly by changing clubs and altering my setup. Once I take my setup, I focus on where I want the ball to land, not the hole. When practicing shots of different trajectories, place towels on the green as your landing spots and develop a feel for picking a club and a shot that will get you to those spots.

—Annika Sorenstam, two-time U.S. Women's Open Champion

The Short of It

If you're not sure about the importance of the short game, don't take my word for it: Keep track of your strokes. Every time you play a shot within 100 yards of the green, mark it on the scorecard and then rate your execution of the shot on a scale of 1 to 5. I bet you'll find two things: You play a lot more shots than you think you do from 100 yards in and your execution is not as sharp as it should be.

Keeping track of your rounds, you'll also find that you're better in some areas than others. You may be a fairly confident chipper, but become a nervous wreck when you have to pitch over sand or water. You may discover that you always take the air route over the

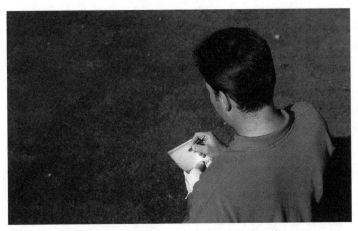

Keep track of your short-game shots and rate them 1 to 5.

BEST TIP: Club Drills

Sometimes the best feedback you can get while practicing comes from a club—not the one you're swinging, but a club on the ground. Here are two simple drills to groove your chipping technique. First, place a club along the outside of your right foot and perpendicular to the target line. With the ball off your right instep, practice chipping balls with the clubhead missing the club on the ground (see photo at right5). Second, create a track for your clubhead with two clubs about four inches apart and aimed at the target. Practice chipping between the shafts to ensure an on-track swing path.

—Martin Hall, *GOLF Magazine*
Master Teaching Professional

---

ground route, or that you have an aversion toward your sand wedge. These are all useful things to know as you look at ways to improve your short game.

Once you know where your weaknesses are, you know where to focus your practice efforts. The old adage "play to your strengths" is wise advice, but around the green you can't always control where your ball ends up. You have to learn how to play all of the basic short-game shots, and that starts with making sure your technique is sound.

Review the basic instruction contained in this book and devise your own improvement plan. Re-

member, practicing just for the sake of practicing is useless. As Dave Pelz puts it in *Dave Pelz's Short Game Bible*, "Practice doesn't make perfect; practice makes permanent. If you practice poorly, you will become consistently poor ... perfect practice makes for good progress and improvement."

To begin with, practice your worst shots first; they're probably causing the biggest disasters on your scorecard. Devote some time to these dreaded shots in every practice session, before you go onto the ones you play with confidence. And for those who say they have no place to practice, think again. You may have to use your imagination, but there's always a way to practice most of the shots in your short game.

Take your own backyard. Okay, so you don't have a practice bunker back there, like some Tour players do, but you can still find plenty to practice. Try pitching over picnic benches or chipping to tree trunks. No doubt you could find some pretty ugly lies in your yard—thick, clumpy lies, maybe even some hardpan. Indoors, try chipping to table legs or clipping specks of dirt off the carpet. These activities are not only fun diversions; they're at your disposal every day. If you look at it this way, the short game is easier to practice than either the full swing or putting. Any other excuses?

Make It Real

While practicing at home can be useful, try to simulate on-course conditions as often as possible when you practice. If your course has a short-game practice area, stake out a spot there and put some time in chipping and pitching the ball various distances from various lies.

At the very least, hit shots from grass cut the same length as the rough you find around your greens. And practice hitting balls from less-than-perfect lies. Without conscious thought, most golfers instinctively roll their practice balls into fluffed-up lies and then feel cheated when they don't get them on the course. One way to create realistic lies is to throw the balls up in the air and play them from wherever they come to rest. In addition, make sure you practice with the same kind of ball you play with. If you prefer a soft-covered ball but practice your short game with range balls, you'll develop two sets of sensations. That's no way to keep it simple.

Another thing that amateurs often fail to do when they practice is attach value to the shots. It's easy to think of every shot as a "freebie" when you practice; after all, just rake over another ball and you can try it again. But instead, try to discipline yourself into thinking that every shot counts. Make up contests for yourself, such as refusing to go home until you chip eight out of ten balls into an imaginary five-foot circle around the hole. Give the shots meaning. Remember, there are no do-overs on the course.

Finally, divide your practice time to mirror your game. For instance, if you shoot around 100, you probably play about 60 shots per round within 100 yards of the green. So spend 60 percent of your practice time on short shots—maybe 30 percent on putting and the other 30 on chipping, pitching, and sand play. To stick to this, spend fifteen minutes on the putting green before you hit the range, then intersperse short wedge shots between every five full swings you make, and end your session in the short-game area. Without a plan like this, your practice sessions will tend to be ball-beating exhibitions. Adher-

Focus your practice by imagining a five-foot circle around the hole.

ing to a plan may take some discipline, but you'll develop a more well-rounded, more satisfying game.

Make It Fun

To many golfers, practicing the short game is about as exciting as watching grass grow. If you're of this mentality, you need to overcome that feeling of drudgery by recognizing the importance of short-game practice and then making it more engaging. As Bobby Jones put it in his famous instructional *Bobby Jones on Golf,* "Practice must be interesting, even absorbing, if it is to be of any use. Monotony palls, and nothing can be more monotonous than playing over and over the same shot from the same place."

To elevate your interest level, strive to create a sense of challenge or competition when you practice by playing a friend or pitting one ball against another. A few simple games for your practice green come to mind: playing a nine-hole match trying to get up and down from various spots around the green; chipping three balls and then putting out your worst effort; pitching one ball and chipping another to the same hole. If you really want to make things interesting, have you and your opponent create each other's lies and designate the club to be used.

> ## Local Knowledge
>
> Does your home course often call for a certain kind of shot? For instance, the greens may be elevated and propped up by steep banks, making the bank shot a useful weapon. If so, practice hitting into steep upslopes whenever you get the opportunity. Or, you may find the need for a specially designed club, such as a lob wedge or a sand wedge with a lot of bounce, to handle situations you commonly encounter. Point is, keep track of the types of greenside shots your course presents and make sure you have the skills and the equipment required to execute them.

That'll test your imagination and your ability to think quickly and manufacture shots.

If you still find short-game practice uninteresting, limit the time of your sessions to ten minutes each. Alternate your practice from putting to full-swing work to the short game, keeping the stimuli fresh by jumping from one to the other before your mind can start to wander. Remember, practice loses

Practice getting up and down: Chip the ball, then try to sink the putt.

its effectiveness when you fall into a routine of just going through the motions. Stay focused.

The Rewards of Hard Work

Progress in your short game comes in two forms: actual and perceived. It cannot be disputed that every golfer can improve his short game with a fair amount of focused practice. If you keep statistics on your rounds, you'll start to see a higher up-and-down percentage, closer putts for par, and generally better scores.

> ## BEST TIP: *Rhythm Method*
>
> Good rhythm is crucial to pitching and chipping. But it's difficult to keep in rhythm if the lengths of the backswing and follow-through don't match. A short backswing causes overacceleration at impact and an overly long follow-through; a long backswing leads to deceleration at impact. Practice making the backward and forward motions equal in length. Once you get a feel for these "mirror-image" motions, your short-game swings will have smooth rhythm, producing solid contact and better distance control.
>
> —Keith Lyford, *GOLF Magazine* Top 100 Teacher

You'll also notice a capability for making quicker, smarter decisions regarding which shot to play in a given situation and which club to play it with. This is a by-product of increased practice: You'll be the proud owner of a better feel for how to manage your short game. That's real progress.

Perhaps even more important is your perceived progress. If you can stand up to greenside shots with the confidence to execute them with a free mind uncluttered by negative or anxious thoughts, your entire game will improve. It's true, a confident short game takes the pressure off the rest of your game. Imagine how much more relaxed you'll feel on approach shots, and tee shots for that matter, knowing you can miss a green and still have a good chance at par. Good feelings can be just as infectious as bad ones.

So get out there and start practicing, because an ability to read and handle greenside situations is the most effective protection against wasted strokes. Practice is the only thing that will get you thinking better, executing better, and therefore scoring lower. Now that sounds like something every golfer should do. Simply put, it is.

As your short game improves, your confidence around the green will soar.